Fighting through hardships
and against all evils;;
We shall find bliss.

L.I.F.E.

L.I.F.E.

Tasnim Alam

Copyright © 2011 by Tasnim Alam.

ISBN: Softcover   978-1-4568-5618-2
                  Ebook   978-1-4568-5619-9

All rights reserved. No part of this book may be reproduced or transmitted in any form or by any means, electronic or mechanical, including photocopying, recording, or by any information storage and retrieval system, without permission in writing from the copyright owner.

This is a work of fiction. Names, characters, places and incidents either are the product of the author's imagination or are used fictitiously, and any resemblance to any actual persons, living or dead, events, or locales is entirely coincidental.

This book was printed in the United States of America.

To order additional copies of this book, contact:
Xlibris Corporation
0-800-644-6988
www.xlibrispublishing.co.uk
Orders@xlibrispublishing.co.uk
301276

Acknowledgements

There were many who helped me with this collection of work. Without some, this book wouldn't have come to exist.

Halima Bibi—without whose watchful eye—these words would have never been written. The girl, who watched over as I wrote my lyrics, gave the odd opinion here and there. Without her personality, her entire being, I doubt that I'd be The person I am today.

Salma Akhtar—her attentiveness at the Birmingham's Young Laureate Short Listing Event gave me the confidence, the belief that I actually had a talent. Even though anyone who knows me will know that I can literally speak for England, I didn't always used to be like this. Moving back to the place in which I was born after eleven years was daunting, there were people I knew, people I didn't know. But I quickly made friends at Park View and they were amazing. This is just one of them.

Sabah Rafique—for having pure faith in me, for never doubting me. It seems as though some people on this earth are destined for greatness and she seems to be one of them. Her personality is one of a kind.

Kasim 'Kaey' Mohammed—Curiously, we started off as enemies, school rivals, who disliked each other because of the simple fact that we thought the other was stuck-up and arrogant. It was actually when we left school that we became quite close. Soon after, he became the person I went to for advice and a critical analyst over my poems. In fact, there's a poem in this collection written by the both of us, titled, *Lies. Indifference. Fear. End.*

Zeba Chowdhury—for her creative inspiration and help in writing the first conversational poem we've written. I think it's amazing how some individuals can stir something up inside you and reveal the greatness within.

Afsana Begum—for showing me a new way of expressing emotions. Like any other teenager, most of my friends split up and went their own ways in this stage of life but never-the-less; she stayed in touch and aspired with me.

Muhsina 'N' Shahid—for being by my side during the whole process. It isn't easy to cope with the stress of having to write a book, with so many deadlines (most by myself) but with a good friend, it really is possible.

Saba Iftikar—for her company during tough times at school that any teenager may experience. This friendship, I must say, influenced what I've written. An amazing person, she makes up in personality for her lack of height.

Shabana Begum—for listening to me spit my bars and giving me encouragement. Another amazing individual that I had the fortune to be friends with.

Members at Park View School

Zahra 'Ticey' Ibrahim—for her encouragement and for listening to me with great patience. I would also like to express gratitude to Zahra for spending her time in reading my *bars*.

Miss Harrell—my secondary school English teacher. An amazing woman within herself. When you first get a look at her, you may actually think she belongs to some sort of gothic cult, but you couldn't be further from the truth. Her English skills are amazing and I believe that she could do better than just teach English, Head of English perhaps?

Mrs Bibaroo—for sacrificing her own study time to help me adjust and improve my first ever poem, *A Way to Lose Me*. Without those few hours, I probably wouldn't have the adrenaline to write anything else. My former mentors, **Wayne** and **Sidra** who both took the time to understand and appreciate my views within my poems. **Mrs Clark**, for supporting me throughout the events of the Birmingham Young Laureate's Short Listing Event.

The Fammalam

My sister for expressing love. Sibling rivalry is one of the many things that I was fortunate not to have. My sister is an amazing person (runs in the genes). I do love her. **My mum** for having faith in me. **My dad** for having confidence in me. Both parents gave what they had with the best of intentions and, for that, I give them my thanks.

Shahanara 'Shara' Begum—the great 'young' aunt—for encouraging and believing in me, for making me see the world in a different way. **Abu Dharr Colin Greengrass** for his humorous poems which played a part in inspiration. **Zaynab Greengrass** for bearing with me while I rehearsed my poems for Birmingham's Young Laureate's Short Listing Event. **Maryam Greengrass**—even though she hasn't noticed it—but her creativity and wide imagination played a part in my inspiration.

Mohammed Sajid Ali—for showing me so much kindness.

Members at the High School

Tyler Heselton for reading my poems from the minute I decided to publish. **Torri Cooper** for listening to me yap in the first few weeks of the autumn term about my poems. **Katt Mann** for making my writing experience a pure laugh and for understanding my point of view. **Cait Boor** for critically reading my poems and encouragement. **Beth Curtis** and **Emily Reed** for the first ever interview about my book.

Mr Haynes for his confidence in me. **Mr Cattal** for allowing me to open up my mind and dig deep into my imagination. **Mrs Fazal** and **Mrs Lipinski** for taking an interest in my work and giving feedback.

A huge thanks to **Mrs Shaw** for introducing me to some *wicked* IT work that came in handy for the pictures on the front cover. Those rushed five minutes made a big impact on the way the book looks the way it does.

Additional Thanks

I would like to thank **Kayleigh Hather, Emma Kirkby, Catherine Rose, Emma Rose, Anita Morgan, Moqadas Khalida, Tanzeala Waqas, Ismail Rauf, Jannatul Yasmine**, and **Fathema Ibrahim** for their time and effort in reading my work.

Any friend who has helped with the photography of the front cover.

Roy Andrews, Marietta Reyes and the rest of the **Xliblris** team for the production of this collection.
Eminem—for his inspirational lyrics; '*the world's on my shoulders.*'
Bruno Mars—Lyrics—'*Just the Way You Are.*'

And Ten.

Contents

Introduction: How It Began 17

Lies. Indifference. Fear. End 19

Text Message...21

Control 22

WEIRD 24

This Life is Yours 25

Life is an Alphabet..27

Media Franchise 28

GCSEs 31

Reach the Stars 33

Three Words, Three Syllables...35

Philadelphia—The Hood To Be At 36

When Love Dies 38

Silenced..39

Ask Yourself.. 40

Revenge 41

Peaceful Battles... 42

What's Around the Corner?.. 43

Normalities 44

Mortals 45

Nostalgia.. 46

Stranger 47

Honest Opinions 48

Ambitions 49

Chillax 50

Medicine 51

The Killer 52

Success 53

Broken Tear Duct 54

From Zahra 'Iicey' Ibrahim: 55

Pledges on Ledges 56

For Mum, Dad and Ramisa;
Though we may be miles apart,
You will always remain locked in my heart . . .

'I will not condemn you for what you did yesterday, if you do it right today.'
Sheldon S. Maye

'You can't have a better tomorrow if you are thinking about yesterday all the time.'
Charles F. Kettering

'Embrace change. True success can be defined by your ability to adapt to changing circumstances.'
Connie Sky

Introduction

When I first wrote those lines,
My skills, I didn't know that I could rhyme,
My mates said *'come on girl, Nimmy,*
Spit them bars, you can grime.'

But without this one person, I wouldn't shine,
That homie's name is Halima Bibi,

I may not believe in besties,
But if I did, she's my trustie,

Now this is how it started:
On a Wednesday afternoon,
At the Naseby Girl's group,
The coppas were visiting the youth,
Talking about jail, court and truth,
And outa nowhere—on the table,
Halima points out— That's for you!'
I go, 'You what?' She goes, 'Yeah, it's true!,
You write the reality. Not what them rappers spit,
Not about useless relationships, money and *bits.'*

I took her advice,
Thought over it a bit,
So I entered them four poems in *Birmingham's Young Laureate.*

And then three months later,
What do you know?
I was shortlisted, asked to come perform for the show,
Told my Aunty, come along let's go,
We hit the road.

Destiny.
I didn't win.
But my world—did it spin?
Look where I am now,
You're holding my book,
Turn the page—have another look.

Thank you girl,
Thank you Haych Beeh x3
Cos' without you,
These words wouldn't have come to life.

Lies. Indifference. Fear. End

Life. Like Eminem's Halie's Song, 'the world's on my shoulders', and everyone's depending on me. Expectations pile up, thoughts anchoring me to this world. Dragging me to the depths of the Pacific Ocean, the crushing disparity of the sea. Bearing down on me, pressurising me. I need reassurance I'm doing the right thing.

Rarely do you feel successful and, when you do, they stop and stare; gleam and glare. 'You ain't achieved what 'we' wanted', confronting you. You ain't good enough, your smile's a bluff. Insults fly like bullets, feeling show, you cover up what you got. But I have to show them.

Loyalty's a joke, honour considered madness.

Crushing on some next girl they met over Facebook, I'll show them my right hook. College, Uni—I'm living my life as to how I want it. Street-lamps die, along with the hopes and dreams of mankind, swallowed by the night. Never to bow down to society, conform to their rules.

Their only option is to dive into a fish pond, stupid and ignorant, like a blonde. I don't care what they say; I'll do what I want each and every day. For the love of God and all His might. I hate that they give a damn, why bother having a fit. Come on, go on. Be a man.

Grow up. Stand tall. Ain't no-one being your mummy—your courts the one with the ball. Stop thinking my life's yours, or else. I'll leave your heart sore, for sure. Knife me? Stab me? Bomb me? Ain't no-one stopping my legacy. The ink of my pen flows like The Nile—never-ending.

I ain't bowing down to you or your level. Try to bring me down, I say no and stand my ground. I'm gonna be huger than life, they'll see me from Mars and Venus.

Wake up and shake off the cobwebs. This ain't back home, this is the West. The old generation's dead. You might end up like that—change is best. Cos you make me sick, make me tick. From your nagging, oh get lost. Quit your beef, cos I'm boss. Let me deflate your big head and see the real you, cos right now, you ain't a true

Exceptionally weird? Yeah that's me.

Text Message

Buzz, buzz.
The phone's news feed,
'New Message'
Quick, you read then re-read,
You don't believe your eyes,
Your text, to you, it lies,
It's a mistake, can't be possible.

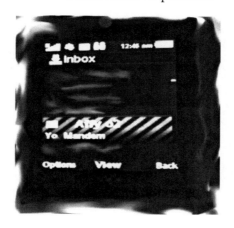

You scream in horror,
Your family say, 'why you holler?'
You say, 'ah nothing, don't bother.'
They raise their eyebrows,
With a confused frown,
Looking like they wonder,
Hey come on, show us what's on your phone . . .

And you do, and smile
Cause it says . . .

*Congratulations.
You have been awarded
Free weekend text and calls from Vodafone.*

Control

Misunderstanding.
They don't get you. They jump to conclusions.
When you try to give an explanation, they don't care.
-To them it ain't true.

Frustration.
It gets you.
Works you up.
They won't stop.
The feeling burns, the heat it creeps.
Makes your neck churn, fidget and turn.
Your mood makes a change.
You've suddenly become stern.
But why do they blame you? Why? Oh why?
This ain't right. You want them jerks outta your sight.

Humiliation.
Someone puts words in your mouth.
Your blood rushes and races again.
You try to keep your head south.
You walk along a corridor,
They spread out; give you way, like trout.
No, not as curtsy but outta mock.
Your unspoken intention just turned into a felony.
You feel like you wanna be a bird; part of a flock.
The insults—the rude remarks; they give you an electric shock.
You want them to shut up;
Bolt their mouths with a padlock.

L.I.F.E.

Mitigation.
Your temperature drops.
Your cheeks go darker then pale.
The idea of violence vanishes and flops.
You know anger ain't the option.
That'll make you fail.
Sometimes you feel regret.
That bitter sensation.
Shoulda passed the reaction, you wish it let.
Will it happen again?
No. To yourself you bet.
But your mind is set;
You will get, those who let you down,
Made your smile turn upside down;
Made your food look like it was brown.

But you don't; cause your world;
You know it'll come crashing down; all the way to the ground.

WEIRD

Weird, what's it mean?

Is it cause your socks are green?
Or is it cause you're not clean, or pristine?

Is it cause you like your teabag in a cup?
Or is it cause instead of saying hello, you say wassup?

Is it cause you brush your teeth after you eat?
Or is it cause you only consume Halal meat?

Is it cause you drink skimmed milk?
Or is it cause you wear gold silk?

Is it cause they call you *chav*?
Or is it cause of something *special* you don't have?

Is it cause you're a young lady and you burp?
Or is it cause you fancy Slim Shady and you slurp?

Is it cause on your pizza you love mushrooms?
Or is it cause you still watch Looney Toons?

Is it cause you must write with your left?
Or is it cause your style looks like you've committed theft?

Is it cause you love fresh fish?
Or is it cause you still sometimes make a wish?

Is it cause you're unique?
If it is, then you don't need a clique.

This Life is Yours

You're bankrupt, your time's up,
Now you collect money in a teacup,
Them thugs walk past, laughing,
Saying wagwan, wassup?
You retort, shut the *buck* up,

You suck on fags, found on the ground,
You live like a tramp, not even on food stamps,
A stray hound, your personality sound,
What else to do? You don't know,
That's what your intelligence shows,

But inside, you know you got more,
So why and for what you keeping it in store?
You're making your own future sore,

On the outside you act hard,
When really, inside you're soft,
Like paraffin and fragile, fish fin,
Don't blame yourself for what's did—it's done,
You ain't the only one, who's committed sin,

Even though you say that to yourself,
You turn around and look back over those years,
They made you feel as though, in a library,
You own your own shelf,
A record of all your bad deeds, so you can't proceed,
But on the contrary,
Was it really that bad?
Is it worth being so sad?

Man, get up, don't be so glum,
Put aside that 30 pence tobacco gum,
You still got your chance,
Maybe one day you'll fly to France,

So don't listen to what they say,
Smile to yourself, today's a fresh new day,
Just hop up and go,
Don't look back and when you shine,
You can say to them, *this life is mine.*

Life is an Alphabet

Adulthood
Babies
Childhood
Depression
Education
Family
Growth
Hormones
Independence
Jobs
Knowledge
Love
Mother
Nosebleeds
Oxygen
Patience
Quarrels
Religion
Siblings
Tax
Uterus
Vengeance
Water
Xbox
Youth
Zealous

Media Franchise

Hourglass figure, high heels, hair curls,
Do not fall in love with these,
For these are what the media hurls,
These counterfeits are only used to deceive,
To not allow what the heart pleases,
But only what the mind releases.

These women in glossy magazines,
Look as if they're dressed for Halloween,
Make-up, fake-up, pose so salacious,
The smiles, the laughs, all bravado,
Behind the face on show,
The truth, the hurt, no one knows . . .

The good, the bad, now impossible to differentiate,
Manipulate the real story, add a word,
Say that you heard it from a little bird, just humiliate!
Media franchise, oh my! What lies!
Sorry Mister Celebrity, you cannot hide!

The man behind the green-screen,
Wears make-up, his real identity unseen,
The winks, the charm, all a façade,
Money his best friend, wow, his life must be hard,
The loneliness, the eagerness is hidden by a poker card.

The latest style must be followed,
Get up! Don't be wallowed,
Be a sheep, follow the herd,
Drift away, become boohai, like a cloud,
Don't be unique, original, or proud.

L.I.F.E.

'Global Warming'—a *catastrophe,*
'Chinese Pollution' made history,
Masonry just given publicity,
'Swine flu,' flew from Mexico to England,
'Catch it, bin it, kill it,'
Why not stick with it?
What next—'World Cup Mayhem?'

The media portrays the truth,
The camera never lies,
We need to know why,
Alexander McQueen committed suicide,
We need to know why,
Sam and Kate's 'Titanic' sank,
We need to know,
The Music Chart's top rank,
The Box Office smash,
We need to know about,
Britain's Next Top Model,
Big Brother and who in Britain's got Talent,

Allow those under seize,
Starving and suffering,
Fighting for their freedom,
Driving for their democracy,
Longing for their liberty,

Forget the hundreds,
Forget the thousands,
Forget the millions—of innocent civilians,
Forget the Economic Recession,
Oh no! Here comes Depression!
But don't worry, here's a copy of '*The Sun,*'
Ha-ha! Yes, you got it, that's a pun,
Rupert Murdoch, you've had your fun.
We buy your news; don't you think we deserve some truth?
Yes, that means there can't be a lack of proof,
We rather see the reality, the brutality,
Regardless of the disturbing images,

Come on! Display the real inhumanity,
The real heroes, the real villains, the real insanity,
Oh Lord! Help this gullible society see reality!

GCSEs

End of August,
Day young people get results of GCSEs,
Some cry and weep,
Some jump and scream with glee,

English, maths, physics, chemistry, biology,
Are they an A* or an E?
Is it what you expected when you left that hall back in May or June?
If not,
Are you going to let it decide whether you're going to be a Uni Student or a Goon?

Best not,
So take that moment as a warning shot,
The bullet hasn't pierced a hole yet,
Get your ass off the couch and away from the T.V. set,

Don't allow those *letters* decide your future,
You won't be a butcher,
You'll be what you dream, top of the cream,
Feeling like a king or queen,
So sit back a bit, relax,
The anger let it away, steam,

The reality has struck, the big life clock ticks, tocks,
So put your head down and put on that thinking crown,
No more messing around, don't be a fool, a clown,

Wait. Wait.
Relax. Relax.
Wait. Wait.

The time approaches,
Come September, the real work begins,
So forget what's written and aim for them stars.

Reach the Stars

You're locked inside, away in a box,
Your opportunities pushed aside,
The time, it ticks, it tocks,

When you're awarded, the bliss, you don't feel the shocks,
When you've achieved a lot,
No one gives a buck,

When you've made a mistake,
They notice, what bad luck!
They hold it against you forever,
Like eggs, you suck,

Why oh'why?
The 21 questions, don't bother answer,
They don't listen to what you say,
They don't care what you think,
Your blurb's just too blunt,
You've made a mistake; your life's been burnt,
How could you pull a stunt?
What crap? You didn't deserve that slap,
Maybe a slight tap—though verbally,
But it was physically,
But now it affects you mentally, emotionally,

The punishment didn't make sense,
Cause and effect,
Not done properly,
What do you do next?
Send your best mate a text?
What they gonna do to save your ass?
You best think on your feet, fast!

So live your life to the max,
Don't wanna end up on the road,
Playing the sax,
Saving money for a fag,
Or becoming cheap,
For a some ol'shag,

Prove them wrong,
Show them your heart song,
      Metaphorically speaking, that is,
Reach the stars, by being who you are.

Three Words, Three Syllables

When you hold me,
Tell me that you'll be there for me till the day I die,
When I shed a tear,
Tell me that everything's gonna be alright,
Even if the truth hurts, try the worst,
I'm stronger than that,
My heart won't burst,

But if this is lust,
Closing all doors on you is a must,
So boy, you best not be unjust,
And think before you say those three words.

Philadelphia— The Hood To Be At

Philadelphia, city of Brotherly Love,
City where Will Smith once stood,

Jay-walk down the block
Crank the music up,
R &B, hip-hop, street rock,

On your walk down Broad Street,
The door of *Dunkin Doughnuts*[1] swings,
Smell of fresh iced tea, oh, so sweet,
A hasty biker on his way,
Crispy bagel—he munches away,
An ordinary street hooligan,
With his friend,
Share a bag of heart-shaped pretzels,

Jump the *Septa*[2] or catch the *El*[3],
A bumpy ride, what the hell?
Go downtown, sight see the *Liberty Bell*[4],
Or visit the Art Museum; learn the city's history,

This place has got so much in store,
Surely, you will never bore, go explore,
Benjamin *Franklin's Institute*[5],
Take a trip to Center City's *Gallery*[6],
Or learn William Penn's voyage route,

Walk along the Delaware River,
The beauty of it will make you quiver,
What a diverse community,
See it yourself at Temple University.

L.I.F.E.

The hood's annual block party,
Grab your friends, have a cook out,
Or pull out the barbecue,
Oh! Can you hear that melody?
-*Wired 96.5FM*, oh snaps! It's Eminem!

Put the flat screen on the street,
Flick on! Click, the Superbowl,
Philadelphia Eagle Show,
Terrel Owen's touch down, woah!
Hustle, bustle for the remote,
MTV! The *Yo Mamma* show!

The sun's about to set,
Is time for B-Ball?
            -You bet!
Shoot some hoops like Allen Iverson,
Go *76ers*, no comparison!

Sun's gone down, no one's around,
Take a break,
Buy yourself a classic Philly cheesesteak,
Or have a snack—*hoagie*, *Lays*, or *Hershey* bars,
Lie down at Penn-Park and just stare at the stars.

Aah! The Philly life,
Perfect place, just so right!

When Love Dies

To, her you're like the dead leaves on the Autumn ground,
She doesn't know where you're bound,
The distance shouldn't have been considered,
The time shouldn't have mattered.

You've made her eyes sore,
From the rain she's poured, from her eyes,
Your million lies, this feeling is now a bore,
From you, she expected more, not this,
No definitely, not this,
She was deceived, offended, amiss.

She wanted your peace, your heart,
She wanted nothing else, but you tore her apart,
Misunderstanding? No she wouldn't call it that,
You didn't even think, now that's a bit daft,
For you—her heart had built up like a blimp, so fat,
But no, no, no, you thought you were some a pimp. *Phat! Phat!*

She realised what you were, you'd think she'd be glad,
Yet why does she sit here complaining, why?
Cause she's sad,
Her friends tell her, buck him; *he's just a pathetic lad,*
But, no, no, no. Not until you're dead.

Silenced

I come from a hood where homies say *wagwan*,
Now I'm at place where there be Barton Street druggy scums,

Similarities; I'll tell you a common some-
There's them kids, them fatherless ones,
And getting HIV. It's now done, all done for fun.
But to me, it's my Brum Town that's the only shining sun . . .

Missing downtown, that bullring,
That buzzing beat, that hot heat,
On a Saturday morning,
Not so sure I miss that roudy scurry
      on Alum Rock Road.
That spicy smell of spicy lamb curry.
Or that hustle, bustle rush of mangies, ew!
Run away! Hurry! Hurry!

Enjoyin that space down Clarence Street, Cathedral,
Charming, err, not so sure.
Sad. Brum Town had so much in store.
Guess I'm off to Gloucestershire to explore
      If beyond what the eye meets, if there's more.
Due to my SAS. I hope I don't get bored.
At least there's ASDA; something I can afford.
Haha, what a pun, sheesh Gloucesterville, cheer up,
Why so glum?
Quit actin like a group of nuns.

Ask Yourself

Are you pure as a bird, D-O-V-E?
Are you soft and caring, L-O-V-E?
Or is you hard as a R-O-C-K?
Like radiation, B-E-T-A?
Is you like a mannequin, F-A-K-E?
Or just big-headed, E-G-G?
Man, you must be F-L-Y as a B-I-R-D,
Even if you's S-H-Y as a B-E-E,
Go O-U-T there and be who you A-R-E,
Don't just sit there and listen to this melody,
Go and jump U-P and clean your teeth.
N-A-W mate I'm jokin,
Y-O-U to whom I'm talkin,
Ha, now your cheeks are R-E-D,
Maybe not, look in the mirror and S-E-E,
And tell M-E, what you B-E,
Is you H-A double P-Y?
Or *Dead and Gone* like J-T and T-I?

Revenge

The salty tears she tastes at the corner of her lips,
May not be large in volume,
But hold enough emotion to flood the tallest of mountains.

Anger, fear, sadness, and sorrow,
All bind together in a bubble of wet salt,
      -and are washed away with the downpour.

But.

Words nor actions will stop the leap,
The leap to bliss,
Back chatter nor any diss,
Will stop nor create a halt,

A kangaroo's jump will take place,
Shock and a kick in the teeth will be apparent,
      In the enemies face.

Watch, watch, watch.

Peaceful Battles

It is not your burden to bear,
Nor is it your burden to share,
Troubles, violence or cruelty,
Not yours but theirs,
Keep to one and allow all others,
Forgive, forget, and do not follow,
Live, let live and leave the hollow,
Strive and succeed for what cannot be succeeded,
Win and shine, rule and grind,
Rasp and rejoice,
Cheer and scream,
Peace you shall find through mists of boiled water steam.

What's Around the Corner?

Death.

We all go through it.
Either know a dead someone or something.
We mourn, we grief . . .
               . . . and if shallow—some feel joy,
What *saddos*.

But some of us act as though we're immortal,
Those who live by the phrase—
        'Life's too short.'

And some of us live carefully,
Perfecting every move, action and speech.
          'You only live once.'
Cliché

Whatever our belief,
We must remember,
Death is not far away.

Normalities

Problems you say . . .
I'll generalise a few—
Tell me—does it not suit at least some of your days?

Broken bridges—we need to cross,
Even though they may be slippery like sea moss.

Stubborn loves we have to deal with,
The fifteenth marriage anniversary marks the fifth.

Frustration with typical families—
Each one is different, holding alien qualities.

A world of many religions that we, with difficult, sustain,
But our friendship we seem to maintain.

Influenced by the media's portrayal,
We live our lives—so insane, as *if* magical.

Friendships fluctuating like the rhythm of a roller coaster ride,
But become calm again like a smart business man's stride.

Jobs—we seek with the highest wage,
But are still unhappy with the numbers on the billing page.

Siblings, we always seem to quarrel,
But then you seem to love each other as well.

Qualifications, the world's obsession,
Politics—the world's love—never links to confession.

So—life's hard isn't it?

Mortals

I'm tired of going around in circles,
Problems trouble me like sharp icicles,
    about to drop—penetrate the membrane,
Becoming like a mop—the nerves explode in the brain.
The noodles slurp and turn into worms,
The venom spreads and the rain, it storms.

You begin to think,
Everyone's acting freaked.
You begin to feel as though-
Your secrets have been leaked.

Who to trust?
Who to bust?
Where to go?
Where to stay?

Life's either accelerating or decelerating,
    no stationary point.
Nothing's simple because it's a complex joint,
But I say—end of the day . . .
You don't live forever.

Nostalgia

Memories, they bring the good,
The laughs, the bad, the tears,
So you don't know if you want to rid them,
Sometimes you want them to vanish on the count of ten.

Otherwise to keep them-
Something to yearn,
Something to smile about . . .

But the same memory can lead to a frown—
You want to shout,
To hit, to pounce, to hurt,
You feel powerless,
Maybe wear a red shirt.
Fire, devil, hell, just *burn*!
Like the centre of the sun.

They mess you around.
The memoirs express the moments—
And sometimes you become hopeful—
hopeful on what becomes *lies*.

Then you feel regret,
Regret for being part of the memory that was created . . .
You begin to wonder *why*?
So to *yourself* you begin to lie.
Like that old saying—'forgive and forget.'

Stranger

Dear Drinker,

Hate was in the air. Love had disappeared. Time—we wait, for bliss to reappear. Feelings and emotions—we lock away, deep in the brain, far in depth; *repress*. Expressing the pain, to the walls, through violence, verbal diarrhoea and more. Loud mental music, bruises to scars, blood stains on your tunic.

What do we do? Who do we confide in? Vomiting over the toilet, the *liquid* bin. You've taken it over to drink and binge. I tell you to take it slow. You ignore me and tell me 'to go.'

A bit fast paced you are there—like this letter—I tell you not to take the weed. You don't care. We both see your yellow or pale reflection in the mirror, we stare.

Who are we? What do you see—your face is like pee—yellow. Now you *know* to listen to me.

With love,

The Conscious xxx

Honest Opinions

Listen.

This is about you my mate,
You don't need to alternate,
Like Bruno Mars says,
You're amazing, just the way you are.

Your appearance doesn't define your individuality,
Your inside beauty is your best quality,
The skies can't beat your personality,
So vast, full of colour,
You're not in need of a parlour.

So just carry on with the things you do,
Ignore everything like a snail's residue.
'Tis all good. You're ample, understood?

Learned.

Ambitions

Think straight, take in every word, properly.
This is the big world, not a game of monopoly.
Take your life seriously,
Though—be lax at times—
Not so melancholy . . .

Don't take in too much pride.
But the success, do not hide.
The haters, watch they'll stand by,
Watching your every move.

Keep your loved ones by your side,
When you've achieved—your goal—do the groove.

You'll be that future light,
No matter what they say,
You'll be that shining knight.
They'll gape at you every day.
You'll be that amazing sight,

No matter how many *moral* fights . . .

Chillax

Like a sea of stars: *Milky Way.*
Go to a dreamy place: *run away.*
Up high with the galaxies: *deep in space.*
Where there is no if or how: *a splendid place.*

Just take a break, clear away with a leaf rake.
Ignore all the problems and situations causing stress,
Some more luxury where there is no possible mess.
Groom yourself, pedicure, manicure, and your hair—*un*tress.

Sometimes—you need time off.

L.I.F.E.

Medicine

Sometimes you just bottle the *stuff* up inside your head,
Like them little kiddies save coins in a piggy bank—
Then suddenly you burst out and your personality becomes rank—
Your charisma has let you down, it shrank—
And your mind; you lost it like when the *Titanic* sank—
Now you just roam around the block with a hood and do your job, daily
    shank.

And it leads to . . .

Making those *renditions*
Getting your share, in a senseless state, you don't care.
Blad, some next missions, Givem' a *touch.*
Then with the dosh, you *buy* something,
Make yourself feel posh, but it's worth nothing,
Next thing, you sell it off,
Whether it's a car, gun or phone,
Because—the *crave,* you *feel* it—the hunger, even in your bones.
Nothing is as important as your cure, your *prescription,*
Authorised by your boss, your *barseman.*
There's no escape, like when cardboard sticks to sellotape.
The separation, the removal is onerous. Almost impossible.

Then there's a black dot in the heart,
From the lies. It grows and grows.
Becomes obese,
Until further it cannot go,
Then you walk back and forth,
Until you slump and cannot stand,
You become pale. And then. There's a smell so stale.

And then the organ dies.

The Killer

Skeleton. With a rifle by its side . . .

The bones—so fragile—yet,
So hard—like stone,
Sharp and dangerous.

But.

Ever so calm,
Unlike the soul,
So relentless and fierce.

The flesh.
Rotted away . . . or eaten.
Food to the worms,
Red to brown to transparency.

Once quick witted.
Now brainless.
Once heartless—but no—
Still heartless.

Eyeballs.
Can't see them.
Blind.
They saw no mercy.
They saw no peace.

Who do *you* see?
Who do *you* imagine?

A soldier.

Success

The money's coming in by the grand per annum,
The money's going out by thousands again,
Like the cardiovascular cycle.

One holiday each year,
Maybe go twice,
To *either* France, Dubai, Denmark or Switzerland,
Or *all.*

The teens, are at private schools,
Then after it's time they go and shoot some pool,
Spending cash by the dozen, hardy harr, what fools.
And then it's poker, gambling and until the jackpot.

An expensive car,
Mercedes-Benz, Lexus, or and if your mental, a *Bugatti.*
Or not.

A daily hired limo,
For your daughter's safety,
The public bus is a prison.

The flow of examples will end now.

Everything is coming in,
Luxuries, 3 course meals and pricey deals.

They're asleep, while the world suffers.
Look at England, now in recession.
Maybe even in the distant future—a depression.

Up and down the VAT,
Down stays the stats,
Cash flow everywhere,
The wealthy, stingy, care to share?

Broken Tear Duct

You know that feeling?
    When a teardrop escapes,
    The corner of your eye,
    Rolls down your cheek,
    And commits suicide off your face?
    I don't remember that feeling.

It's as if the tears have gathered,
My brain secretly sending messages,
    To my tear duct,
    Don't transfer the tears,
Well it's a damned shame,
That feeling used to ease the pain—*a little.*

Only one occasion,
Where the tears are *forced,*
    To fight and escape,
The burning sensation from greasy onions.
Hilarious, how I don't remember that feeling either.

Queer. How that was a medicine for pain,
Yet, it's gone, and a substitute must be found,
A little laughing *gas* may help . . . or—
    Wake me up from this drastic nightmare.

Haha—huhu—hehe.

From Zahra 'Jicey' Ibrahim:

Inspired

Tasnim is my inspiration,
My causation—
My temptation.

I started off with a demonstration,
Tasnim was like an application,
Waiting for my declaration.

Soon enough, it was like a vibration,
Buzz Buzz, *there goes my phone,*
It's Tasnim, my girl.

Yo! This girl got flow,
She's an American Crow,
Don't get me wrong, she was like WOAH!

Lyrics come from the heart,
I know that her work was art,
Coming out soon,
When there's a harvest moon . . . an opportune.

Zahra, *get in there fam.*

Pledges on Ledges

Unbroken promise . . .
A giggle here, laughter there,
A snort escapes her nose,
Trying to hide the mirth,
    In an aching stomach.
Tears begin to roll,
Eyelashes soaked.
A burst prepares to explode,
Like a bomb.
All eyes turn on her,
She conceals her face under her arm,
But shakes slightly,
Laughing to herself,
Slowly, she calms down,
Face turning from red to brown . . .

A message came through the messenger,
Her mouth dropped in disbelief,
All signs of glee hidden behind a face of confusion,
Feeling lost, wondering,
Why? How? Nah, not true . . .
Later on, the message came,
Directly came, from himself,
One syllable, *yh.*
Bravado came on, the laughter back,
But missing a tone—and no aching stomach.
No warm tears or thick soaked eyelashes . . .
No snorts or outbursts,
And no eyes turned on her.
A smile here, a laugh there . . .

Promise broken.

Life is kinda *stinky*.

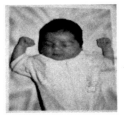 Tasnim Alam was born in Birmingham, England and moved over to America while still a toddler. After eleven years of education in the outskirts of Philadelphia she flew back to England with her extended family. She stayed in Birmingham for a period of almost three years for her secondary school life and then moved to Gloucestershire, where she currently lives, doing her A-Levels.

Lightning Source UK Ltd.
Milton Keynes UK
29 March 2011

170088UK00001B/21/P